THERE'S MORE TO LIFE THAN PUMPKINS, DRUGS and OTHER FALSE GODS

Ken Reiners

Woodland Publishing Company, Inc.
Wayzata, Minnesota

THERE'S MORE TO LIFE
THAN PUMPKINS, DRUGS
and
OTHER FALSE GODS

Copyright © 1980 Kenneth G. Reiners

Library of Congress Catalog Card No. 80-50424

International Standard Book No. 0-934104-03-4

MANUFACTURED IN THE UNITED STATES OF AMERICA

THERE'S MORE
TO LIFE THAN
PUMPKINS,
DRUGS
and
OTHER
FALSE GODS

Acknowledgements

I am grateful to the following:

Sr. Mary Madonna, Chief Executive Officer, St. Mary's Hospital, who hired me five years ago and made possible my experience in the Adolescent Chemical Dependency ministry.

Sr. Rita Clare, Vice President of Patient Services, for graciously tolerating my earthy humanity and unorthodox beliefs.

Fr. Robert Patterson, Director of Pastoral Care, who supported me in writing this book and was always a friend when I needed him during my spiritual depressions.

Elton Ryberg, friend and peer, who gave me the "King Baby" idea for my first chapter.

Helene Reiners, wife, lover and friend, who shared my sorrows and joys the past twenty-two years of my spiritual pilgrimage.

All my friends and staff from the Adolescent Chemical Dependency Unit, who have helped restore me and my family to sanity so we could once more experience joy.

The gracious, caring Sisters from the Home of The Good Shepherd, who provided me with an ideal retreat for writing and who also spoiled me.

Barbara Ladd, friend and editor.

Contents

To our
two children
who are recovering
from the disease of chemical dependency
because they turned their will and their lives
over to the care of God as they understand him.

Foreword

If life is a journey or process, there is no time during that trip which is more difficult and painful than the years of adolescence. For the adolescent who is struggling with the disease of chemical dependency in addition to the normal stresses of growing up, life is filled with chaos and conflict.

This book is concerned with the problems we face in trying to make some sense out of the pain, struggle and loneliness we all endure during our journey. How do we compensate for these experiences and not only survive but actually find some joy and peace while walking this road?

The young people for whom this book is written, are trying to find the answers to these questions by evading the quest. They are escaping into drug induced fantasies. Avoidance of reality is being attempted through a series of self-generated and chemically induced delusions. The end point of this process is a life filled with increased loneliness, conflict and confusion, both for the adolescents and for their families.

The conclusion reached in this book is the same one discovered by St. Augustine in his life centuries ago. We are made for God, and we will never find ourselves or the peace that we seek, until we find God. It is interesting that in his own youth, Augustine followed destructive paths similar to those followed by these young people.

If the discovery of the reality of God is what this journey, this life is ultimately about, how do we find it? Medically we know that a fully operational and functional brain is essential to the maturing process. When we have a young, developing brain that is not able to function and develop normally because of the effects of alcohol and other drugs the outlook for the future is grim.

If discovering God is the answer, and the inability to do that is the problem, what then do we do?

When we are lost we look for help from others. We can't do it alone. We can't do it when we are drunk or high. We need to know we can be loved and accepted. By finding relationships with others, discovering the 12 steps of A.A., and living them, we can make sense out of this existence. We can experience peace and true joy in the process.

This is the message of this book. It is for the young people enmeshed in their struggle and for those who love them and want to help but don't know how.

George A. Mann, M.D., Director
Adult Chemical Dependency Program
St. Mary's Rehabilitation Center
Minneapolis, Minnesota

Preface

Chemical dependency is a wholistic disease. It has no boundaries. Several years ago we thought of alcoholism or chemical dependency as an adult disease. That is no longer true. A problem of epidemic proportions in *every* community today is teenage alcoholism.

In 1975, when I began my ministry as chaplain to the Adolescent Chemical Dependency Treatment Program in St. Mary's Hospital, Minneapolis, Minnesota, alcohol was the primary or secondary drug of abuse with approximately 10 per cent of our clients between the ages of 14 and 18. Currently, alcohol has become the primary or secondary drug of abuse with approximately 70 percent of our young clients. Even more alarming is the fact that one-third or more of our clients are fourteen years old or younger. We are developing a nation of younger and younger alcoholics.

Alcoholism or chemical dependency is wholistic in the sense it affects the whole person—physically, emotionally, intellectually, socially and spiritually. In 1974, St. Mary's Hospital developed the first adolescent chemical dependency treatment program in a hospital setting, to help young people recover from their addiction to alcohol and other drugs. I was privileged to be one of the first chaplains to St. Mary's Adolescent Treatment Program, and minister to the spiritual need of these young people. As I help them clarify, sort out and define God as they understand him, I am aware that most of the literature they receive in their book packets on God and spirituality, is geared toward adult level. This prompted me to write a book on a level that youth can understand, a book that presents the major principles and ideas essential to a spiritual recovery from the disease of chemical dependency. In most cases, the text is written in first person plural and speaks of God, "as we understand Him."

I have written my text in this manner because I believe our spiritual journeys are universal. Most of us are in search of a God of Greater Meaning. We may have different names for God—Jehovah, Buddha, Allah, Great Spirit—or understand God differently, but the journeys we take in search of God are similar. There seems to be an urge or force within each of us that leads us to search for a God of Greater Meaning, a power beyond us, who can bring us peace of mind and joy in a chaotic, troubled and suffering world.

Of 180 high school students interviewed in a suburban high school near Chicago, 178 said the number one problem for a teen-ager in America today is *boredom*. Boredom is a sign of spiritual disease and lack of meaning in what appears to be a meaningless world. It is my hope that this book will guide young people on their spiritual journeys in search for a God of Greater Meaning who can fill their lives with joy!

Ken Reiners

1. King Baby Plays God

King Baby Plays God

None of us shows up in the world with God built-in or even with a built-in devotion to God, but *only* with a built-in devotion to the world itself.[1]

The Parables of Peanuts — Robert Short

Every human relation is joyless in which the other person is not sought because of what he is in himself, but because of the pleasure he can give us and the pain from which he can protect us. . . . To seek pleasure for the sake of pleasure is to avoid reality, the reality of other beings and the reality of ourselves.[2]

The New Being — Paul Tillich

As infants, we were totally dependent on our parents for all our wants and needs. They fed us, changed our diapers and wiped our noses. We learned that whenever we wanted or needed something, all we had to do was cry. Soon Mom or Dad, with smiling faces, would come running to the rescue.

We were like Kings who ruled the family kingdom. We felt powerful. Mom and Dad were our servants and treated us like royalty. In most cases, we got what we wanted when we wanted it.

As we mature we do not outgrow the need to be the center of attention. We still want to be King. We want to believe that we are masters of our fate and captains of our souls.

But we are fooling ourselves. It's like we are sitting in a baby stroller with a play steering wheel. Mom or Dad pushes the stroller and we think we are driving. As long as we turn the steering wheel to the right and Mom or Dad turns the stroller in the same direction, we are content. But if we turn left and Mom or Dad turns right we become angry. We didn't get to go where we wanted.

King Babies trust only themselves. In fact, they think they are God. They worship themselves and believe that no person or thing is as powerful as they are. King Babies care only for themselves and have little concern about who they hurt as long as they get what they want when they want it.

Self-worship or playing God works for a while. But gradually we learn that mother or father is a separate person—not a part of ourselves. We discover that we do not rule the world by our whims and whimpers. Other persons exist in our world and are not in our control. This discovery is called *otherness*.

Of course, the discovery of otherness is only partial. The temptation to be the center of our universe is so strong that we think of others only as an enlargement of ourselves. They are to be jockeyed or juggled according to our wants.

When we fail to discover otherness we tend to treat God as a part of ourselves—a Dad or Mom who rushes to our side whenever we want our wishes granted. But it backfires on us.

Caring only for ourselves (not worrying about anyone else's wishes, or how many people we hurt, disappoint or offend) only leads to failure. Self-serving interests drive friends away. We feel lonely and empty.

Without friends there's no one to trust and we feel helpless and out of control when other events in life, like illness, death, or tragedy, strike us. Alienation from our friends and families causes loneliness and takes away King Baby's fun. Our need for care and support from our families and friends when we experience suffering now becomes more important than our desire to be King Baby.

But where do we turn if we have alienated ourselves from our families and friends? How do we fill the emptiness and nurture the loneliness in our lives? We search for a god, a power greater than we are to help us out of our predicament. We search for someone or something that can bring meaning to our sorrowing lives.

2. Pumpkins, Drugs and Other False Gods

Pumpkins, Drugs and Other False Gods

One of the roots of the desire for pleasure is the feeling of emptiness and the pain of boredom following from it. Emptiness is the lack of relatedness to things and persons and meanings: it is even the lack of being related to oneself. Therefore, we try to escape from ourselves and the loneliness of ourselves, but we do not reach the others and their world in a genuine relation. And so we use them for a kind of pleasure which can be called "fun." But it is not the creative kind of fun often connected with play; it is rather, a shallow, distracting, greedy way of "having fun."[1]

The New Being—Paul Tillich

King Baby alienates us from persons, values and meanings that can fill our troubled and empty lives. Playing God only magnifies our loneliness and sorrow. So we begin to seek other ways to help escape the pain.

In our search to find someone or something of Greater Meaning we are attracted to the pleasures in our world. There is instant relief from pain through coffee, sex, food, booze, drugs, gambling, etc. And they easily become Number One in our lives. Our search for a God of Greater Meaning is detoured. We worship another false idol.

These wretched idols, whether they be pumpkins, drugs or other false gods do not relieve loneliness or sorrow. They only help us escape. We may think we feel happy but when the high is over, the loneliness and sorrow return.

Alcohol and other drugs, for example, can become powerful gods. Abuse of these drugs causes us to love the high. And loving the high becomes so important that these phony gods become the center of our lives. Highs are more important than anything or anybody. Everything we once valued—like parents, brothers, sisters, school, work, virginity—are sacrificed for the sake of the high.

Charles Schultz, in one of his *Peanuts* cartoons shows Lucy saying to Charlie Brown, "WHY CAN'T MY LIFE BE ALL 'UPS'?... WHY CAN'T I JUST MOVE FROM ONE 'UP' TO ANOTHER 'UP'? WHY CAN'T I JUST GO FROM 'UP' TO AN 'UPPER-UP'? I DON'T WANT ANY 'DOWNS!' I JUST WANT 'UPS' AND 'UPS' AND 'UPS!'" This is the way we feel when we become addicted to the highs of drugs. We want to remain with the highs forever.

But life is not that way. With the highs also come lows. Our instant-relief gods, powerful as they are, only satisfy us temporarily. And when we come down from our mountains of "supreme happiness" we discover that our false gods have only postponed our pain of loneliness and sorrow.

Paul Tillich, a famous theologian and church father, speaks of sorrow and joy in his book, *The New Being*. He describes sorrow as the "feeling that we are deprived of something that belongs to us and is necessary to our fulfillment." This could mean being deprived of freedom, family, friends, love or whatever brings meaning and fulfillment to our lives. "Joy," says Tillich, "is possible only when we are driven towards things and persons because of what they are and not because of what we can get from them."[2]

Therefore, King Baby, pumpkins, drugs and other false gods may give us temporary pleasure and relief from pain, but not joy. Joy comes when we are fulfilled by persons or values that can bring greater meaning or fulfillment to our lives.

If we do not learn how to cope honestly with sorrow, we experience no joy in our lives and we die spiritually. Our lives become hollow and empty, "signifying nothing." Our false gods can no longer rescue us or block out the agony of sorrow. However, sorrow can be faced if we are willing to let go of our false idols. By letting go of our false gods and surrendering to a power greater than we are, we can learn from sorrow and grow stronger. In fact, sorrow can be one of our most intimate teachers, moving us toward the restoration of wholeness.

3. On Letting Go of King Baby

On Letting Go of King Baby

As children bring their broken toys,
With tears for us to mend;
I brought my broken dreams to God,
Because he was my friend.
But then instead of leaving him,
In peace to work alone;
I hung around and tried to help,
With ways that were my own.
At last I snatched them back and cried,
"How can you be so slow?"
"My child," he said, "What could I do?
You never did let go!"
                                        —Anonymous

God's word is a summons to reality.[1]
A Reason to Live! A Reason to Die!
—John Powell

Life is filled with broken dreams. Divorce, disease and death
are just a few of life's harsher realities that leave us feeling lonely
and empty. When we experience these "up-against-it" moments
we sense the need for a power greater than ourselves to bring
meaning and hope to our sorrow. In fact, many people seem to
turn to God for help in crises. During times of war for example,
few soldiers facing death in fox holes do not believe in God.
They pray for God to "save" them from death.

Unfortunately, many of us cling to the false security of pumpkins, drugs and other idols instead of letting go of them to allow
God to work alone in peace. And if God or our false gods fails to

rescue us, we often give up on them and attempt to play God by ourselves. We turn to King Baby.

However, true peace of mind comes when we let go of the emotional garbage that we used as King Baby. Letting go is an important ingredient in experiencing a God of Greater Meaning. It's impossible to allow a God of Greater Meaning to fill our lives with joy and peace if we cling to emotional garbage—garbage that belongs to our past.

Letting go of King Baby has many aspects. One is giving up our desire to always be in control of ourselves. Few of us want others to think we are helpless or weak. Therefore, we compensate by acting like we are all-powerful and all-knowing. Some writers have labeled this defense false pride.

How often have we heard, "Be a man!", "Big boys don't cry!", "Keep a stiff upper lip!", "Pull yourself up by your bootstraps!", or "Stand on your own two feet!"? These messages reinforce the myth that we should be always in control of ourselves.

However, this "stinkin' thinkin'" implies that weakness is bad and only a super-human race should survive. The result: we would rather die than admit our weaknesses or faults. Furthermore, desire to be in control of ourselves negates any feelings of disappointment, despair, and defeat. These feelings are important! After all, God created us with the ability to feel so we can relieve tension caused by the strain of living in a stressful world.

To deny feelings is to deny the God of Meaning who created those feelings. And to deny God is to act like King Baby. When we attempt to always be in control of ourselves or our situations we begin to live in fear and be defensive. We fear that others will reject us if we say the wrong words. We fear failure as a lover or as a student. We fear that someone will discover our secrets. Sometimes fears of weakness and failure become so powerful that we end up being afraid of almost everything.

Some of these fears are real, based on past experience. Maybe we told a friend a secret and he or she betrayed our trust and gossiped to others. We were hurt, and rightfully so. Since nobody is perfect, that risk of getting hurt is present in any human situation. However, fear of rejection leads to the loneliness and sorrow which is more painful than the risk of getting hurt one more time. Just as some fears are real, others are unfounded. Often these fears are caused by nothing more than allowing our minds to run wild, thus misreading events and actions of others. For example, someone may misinform us that psychiatrists and counselors in chemical dependency treatment programs brainwash their patients. If we are a patient in such a program we may become so fearful of being brainwashed, we will be unable to trust those persons who are essential to our recovery. Projection of our fears, real or otherwise, becomes another form of controlling our future and ourselves.

Remember: God controls the future; we don't. And our unwillingness to trust God or others makes us cling to our fears. We become paralyzed. This often leads to failure. And that was our fear in the beginning.

Not only do we attempt to control the future, we try to control our past. Evidence of this is heard in expressions like, "If only I had . . . .", "I wish I had . . . .", "I should have . . . .", "Why did I . . . .?" By saying these phrases, we are expressing guilt for not having met an ideal or goal. Our *ideal* self and our *actual* self are at war. Who should we be and who *are* we? What should we do and what are we *actually* doing?

Failure to achieve our own high expectations leads to misery and self-hatred. But self-acceptance—accepting our limits along with our strengths—allows us to be human. And being human is being imperfect. A famous student of mythology, Joseph Campbell, once remarked: "Both artist and lover know that perfection is not love. It is the clumsiness of a fault that makes a person lovable . . . Balance comes as a result of leaning on your faults . . . Where you stumble and fall, there you find the gold."[2]

If we cannot forgive ourselves for being imperfect, we deny the need for an all-forgiving, all-loving God. A God of Greater Meaning gives us permission to fail and to learn from mistakes. Failure to forgive ourselves puts us in a position to be more powerful than God. By not forgiving what God forgives, we are trying to assume a more powerful position than God's.

Letting go of King Baby has another aspect: other people. As King Baby we learned to be self-centered. We con and abuse others to get our wishes granted. We use threats, ("If I can't have what I want I will run away from home!"); blame, ("It's your fault!"); guilt, ("You don't love me!"); generalizations, ("Everybody is doing it!"); and other con games to get our way. When we don't get what we want we hold grudges and therefore, keep people we need for support at a distance.

Sometimes impatience plays a role in our attempts to control others. We want our demands to be answered immediately. But impatience can lead to frustration and defeat. The darkest hour of the night is just before dawn. Many of us fail to achieve our goals because we give up during the "darkest hour." We didn't have the patience to wait or the courage to face any other answer but "yes."

Letting go means waiting or accepting a "no" answer. Sometimes when we let go of what we want *right now* we are given that very thing. For example, my counselor suggests I may have to go to long-term treatment if I don't get honest and responsible in my program. But I am dead-set on going home. If I give up my preoccupation with going home when I want to and become honest and responsible in my program of recovery now, I may not need long-term treatment. Attempting to control others by our impatience destroys those surprises. But letting go of our impatience adds joy, curiosity and surprise.

Impatience is not the only way to control other people. Some of us enjoy self-pity and won't let go of it. We feel sorry for ourselves when we fail to get what we want. We feel helpless by failure. Since King Baby does not like to feel helpless or powerless, we try to fool others into believing we are victims.

In some respects we act like a killdeer. A killdeer is a bird that pretends injury to distract hunters from her eggs. Feeling sorry for ourselves is a way to pretend injury so others will not discover our real feelings of helplessness or hurt. Furthermore, self-pity tricks others into doing our work for us. As infants we would cry and our mothers would hurriedly ask, "Poor baby, what do you want?", and fix the problem for us. We enjoy having other people baby us. And we hate giving that up. As King Baby we play a game called Poor-Helpless-Me and feign injury so others will take responsibility for us. When offered an opportunity to solve the problem on our own, King Baby rejects any possible solution.

This Poor-Helpless-Me game is a hard one to stop playing because it allows us to be the center of attention. We reject help by making up excuses about why our friend's suggestions of help won't work. We convince ourselves it's better to receive negative attention than to be ignored or to face what we really need to do to help ourselves.

Rejecting feedback from our friends soon leads to alienation and loneliness. Friends are hurt by rejection of their ideas. Before too long our friends leave us alone. Self-pity separates us from friends and our real values.

Self-pity also leads to blame. We argue, "But my parents are too strict!", or "I'm too fat!", or "Nobody loves me!" But blame never solves anything and it rarely helps us feel better. In fact, we may feel worse because blame usually causes feelings of resentment. These resentments build up, anger results, and we lash out against others.

It's like carrying a gunnysack on our back. Every time we feel anger towards someone, rather than be honest about our anger, we throw a grudge in our gunnysack. We imagine ways we can get even with the person by slashing his tires or egging his home. Our gunnysack soon overflows with resentments. To rid ourselves of the weight, we dump our bag of grudges on someone nearby. This gunnysacking is a way our King Baby controls others. It appears to be a safe method to disguise our hurt or disappointment. But it's not.

Letting go of our King Baby, of our ploys to control others and ourselves, is hard. Joy, surprise, and a sense of self-worth comes when we become responsible for our own behavior and actions. We convert our love of power to the power of self-love. This is called growing up.

4. On Letting Go of Pumpkins, Drugs and Other False Gods

On Letting Go of Pumpkins, Drugs and Other False Gods

It is ironic that man should feel such a painful void inside of himself when he lives in a world of so many things which fill the air with sound, light and smog, but which apparently cannot fill the heart of man. . . Becoming a person, . . . involves the sacrifice of some experiences in order to experience more deeply the values which are connected with and which promote one's own destiny.[1]

A Reason to Live! A Reason to Die!
—John Powell

Growing up means saying good-bye to our King Baby garbage *and* our intellectual garbage. If we honestly examine our past experiences and ideas of God learned in childhood, we will discover that many of them are far too inadequate and of little value except to reinforce our King Baby behavior. In fact, many of our ideas of God were learned from others with King Baby attitudes.

Psychology experts tell us that our ideas about God are formed in the first seven years of life and were learned, in most cases, from our parents. Furthermore, how we relate to our parents is often similar to the way we relate to God. For example, if our mother or father was strict and always told us what or what not to do, then our God is probably like that. With that upbringing, we may relate to God in an over-dependent manner, fearing we may not do God's will perfectly. This idea of God excludes our humanness and the need for a forgiving God.

If we grew up with parents who were domineering, had all the answers, and made us feel that every idea we suggested was stupid, then our God may be domineering and think we are stupid. We usually relate to this kind of God in fear and shame. This relationship with God excludes a caring, accepting God who loves us just as we are.

Some parents try to please their children or win their affection by always giving them what they want. If we had parents like that we may relate to God as we do Santa Claus, thinking God will give us presents if we are good all year long. We believe God is great if we receive what we ask for in our prayers. If our prayers go unanswered however, we may react in Huckleberry Finn's manner. He prayed to God for a fishing pole and hooks. When he received only the pole he gave up on God and prayer. A God of Greater Meaning is generous and giving. But God does not always give us what we want when we want it. God gives us what we need—understanding, acceptance, forgiveness and care. These gifts are greater than any material gifts.

Some of us grew up with parents who bailed us out of predicaments, even situations caused by our irresponsible behavior or attitude. From these experiences we learn to bargain with God and relate to God like we would a Red Cross Nurse. Our prayers may sound like this: "God, if you get me out of this mess, I'll start attending church more often." Bargaining with God is childish and usually gets us in more trouble. If God fails to rescue us we feel anger and resentment towards God. If it appears God rescues us and we fail our part of the bargain, we feel guilt and shame, and are afraid to approach God. In both ways we lose. We block out God's loving care by our negative feelings.

Many of us grew up believing God is white and male because we grew up in a white, male dominant environment. For some of us, the first prayer we were taught to memorize was, "Our Father, who art in heaven . . ." And how do we understand and experience our heavenly father except through the way we understood and experienced our earthly father? This kind of understanding of God excludes the feminine qualities of God and other races. A God of Greater Meaning includes both male and female—God includes all.

This is not intended to discount our child-like beliefs in God but to illustrate how our past experiences condition, limit and prejudice our understanding of God. By letting go of our exclusive ideas of God we open ourselves to a God of Greater Meaning.

Finally, we experience a God of Greater Meaning when we let go of our false material gods—our worship of Pumpkins, Drugs and other pleasure gods that seduce us. But letting go is hard to do because these gods have relieved some of our pain. We also feel safe with them. They don't criticize us, yell at us or make us obey some "silly" rules. Sometimes our false gods make us feel all-powerful and all-knowing. When high on drugs, some people act more powerful than they do when sober. By overeating, some people feel bigger than others.

However, the pleasure we reap from our false gods is soon overwhelmed by the sorrow of spiritual death. We become suspicious of strangers and keep our friends at arm's length because we fear losing control. We are afraid to play lest we risk appearing like a fool. We don't cry when we are lonely or hurt because we fear others will say we are too sentimental. We are so busy managing the future and worrying that others will find out about our past that we cannot enjoy the present.

We fear failure more than we love life and adventure. Therefore, we fail to take risks which may lead us to a life of surprise, creativity, mystery, meaning and joy. A poet who chose to remain anonymous speaks to this situation: "The person who risks nothing—does nothing, has nothing and is nothing. He simply cannot learn, feel, change, grow, love, live. Chained by his certitudes, he is a slave. He has forfeited freedom."

By risking nothing we may avoid pain but we do not escape loneliness and sorrow. By worshiping false gods we become slaves to sorrow and sacrifice the greater values of life. We forfeit our freedom to discover a God of Greater Meaning.

5. Journey into Powerlessness and Sorrow

Journey into Powerlessness and Sorrow

There will be a new moral conflict,
   a new personal problem,
   a new human relationship,
   a new responsibility to be borne,
   or a new decision to be made.
There is such a deep hunger. . . for God that
   even if the renewed attraction of God
     is pushed aside,
  it will return again,
    perhaps even stronger,
    more deeply moving,
    or more inwardly disturbing.[1]

A Reason to Live! A Reason to Die!
—John Powell

Pumpkins, Drugs and other false gods make us feel powerful. They help us escape pain and provide us with pleasurable fantasies and feelings. But our false gods only become crutches for courage. They hide our real feelings. As Linus says of his precious security blanket, "Only one yard of outing flannel stands between me and a nervous breakdown." False gods build a false sense of security. They alienate us from cherished friends and families, our higher selves, creative values and a God of Greater Meaning. The result: spiritual bankruptcy.

False gods are cunning and baffling. They fool us into believing that all we need from life are pleasurable highs and getting what we want when we want it—at any price. But it's only a fantasy. Life is not that way.

Life is filled with events called crises. These crises are more powerful than our false gods. They shatter our feelings and fantasies of pleasure. Crises or suffering lead us into a journey of powerlessness and sorrow where even our false gods fail to rescue us. Only a power greater than we are, a God of Greater Meaning, can restore us to sanity and fulfillment.

Suffering is part of being human. As long as we live suffering will be a part of our experience. It cannot be avoided. We live in a world of earthquakes, tornadoes, hurricanes and floods. It is a world of incurable diseases and deadly viruses. Some persons are born blind, deaf, dumb or crippled. Others suffer from concentration camps, brutalities, inequality and injustice. Our world is one of obliteration bombing, massacres and mushrooming clouds over cities. We experience failure, retreat and tragedy.

Suffering, for some, seems very unfair. And it is. Because suffering seems to come to some persons in different measure. For some, it comes as an occassional crisis; for others, suffering seems to be a constant companion. However, from suffering or crises, no one escapes. And even though we attempt to avoid the sorrow that comes from suffering by clinging to the false security of our idols, in time it finds us.

For example, breaking the law and being sentenced to jail is a crisis that can help us get in touch with our sorrow. God does not prefer that we go to jail. God prefers that we be responsible and accountable for our behavior. If we go to jail, however, God will use our helplessness or powerlessness to help us grow wiser and more responsible. Sitting in jail gives us time to straighten our priorities and get us in touch with our sorrow—the loss of freedom.

Being inflicted with an incurable disease like chemical dependency or cancer can be a powerful force that gets us in touch with our greater values and helps us develop our higher selves. The crisis of illness can be an opportunity for reflection, new insight and growth. When suffering from illness, we experience sorrow—the loss of good health. Again, God does not want us to become ill, but God will allow our crisis to shatter the fantasies of our false gods so we can recognize the need for a greater power who can restore us to wholeness. Our journeys into sorrow help us discover that things, once important to us, have lesser value and meaning in suffering.

Dr. Elizabeth Kubler-Ross, a famed physician who devoted many years to the study of the experiences of dying persons, speaks of the meaning and greater values that people discover when they are dying. In an interview she said:

> It is very interesting when you look back at hundreds of dying patients—young and old. Not one of them has ever told me how many houses she had or how many handbags or sable coats. What they tell you of are very tiny, almost insignificant moments in their lives—where they went fishing with a child or they tell of mountain-climbing trips in Switzerland. Some brief moments of privacy in an interpersonal relationship. These are the things that keep people going at the end. . . They remember little moments that they had long forgotten and they suddenly have a smile on their faces. And they begin to reminisce about little memories that make their whole lives meaningful and worthwhile. I never understood in 40 years what the church tried to teach—that there is meaning in suffering—until I found myself in this situation.[2]

Death and dying are two of the most powerful crises that intensify our powerlessness and sorrow. They help us get in touch with our need for a power beyond us. A God of Greater Meaning will use dying and death to help us find life's greater values like play, interpersonal relationships, "little moments" and memories that make life worthwhile.

A 19th century philosopher, Frederich Nietsche, who claimed he did not believe in God, once said: "He who has a why to live can bear almost any how." In other words, the person who finds meaningful reasons for living can bear almost any suffering or crisis situation. I know of no other place or time where I've experienced God's loving care more powerfully than in moments of my greatest sorrows and losses. God, others and our greater values can give us "whys to live" when we think we have no other reason for living. True joy is experienced when we surrender to reality—powerlessness and sorrow—and allow God's loving care through others to heal our heartaches.

The crisis of suffering can become a powerful and positive force that shatters the fantasies and false hopes our phony gods give us. The Chinese language has a double meaning for the word "crisis." Crisis can mean both danger and opportunity. The sorrow that comes from the crises we encounter can either cause us to grow bitter and die spiritually or provide us with an opportunity to grow wise, open and gentle. Joy is experienced then, by those who are able to let go of King Baby and other false gods and surrender to God's loving care.

It's like the old Aesop Fable of the sun and the wind competing to remove a man's coat. The wind blew and blew. The more it blew, the tighter the man gripped his coat to shut out the chilling wind. But when the sun came out and warmed the man with it's rays, his coat fell off automatically because he felt a greater warmth from the sun than he did from himself.

If we can let go of King Baby or other false gods, we automatically receive more energy to deal with reality. By letting go of the energy we use to control ourselves, our situations and other people, we open ourselves to a God of Greater Meaning who can warm and fill our hearts with joy.

The false gods we create may give us pleasure and temporary relief from pain, but will also shut out joy. Worshiping false gods alienates us from the realities of powerlessness and sorrow. We exhaust our energies in attempts to block out the harsher realities of life. But when we block out feelings of powerlessness and sorrow we also cut off our feelings of joy. The defenses we learn from King Baby and other false gods alienate us from our body's messages. We may think we experience joy, but we do not genuinely feel it.

True meaning and joy come to those who can find their way into the real world and are willing to journey into powerlessness and sorrow. Sorrow is not an enemy but a journey—a systems movement towards restoration of wholeness and fulfillment. In sorrow we experience the loving presence of God who re-unites us with our higher selves, other persons and a God of Greater Meaning.

6. Journey Out: A Guide to Spiritual Recovery and a God of Greater Meaning

Journey Out: A Guide to Spiritual Recovery and a God of Greater Meaning

Spiritual growth is the key to all human growth. . . . Spiritual growth-work aims at liberating the "vertical dimension" of our lives. It seeks to liberate our belief systems, our values and our relationship with God so that our lives will become more open to these deep wellsprings of growth. We human beings are creatures who live in our hope and meanings and in our beliefs about what is ultimately real and significant. [1]

Growth Counseling—Howard J. Clinebell

Shortly after an atomic explosion several years ago on the desert flats of New Mexico, one of the bomb's inventors exclaimed: "I am a frightened man. All the experts I know are frightened." While waiting for the explosion these "experts" reportedly held their faces to the ground fearing their own self-destruction.

We live in an age in which we have mastered many mysteries of the universe through our scientific genius. "Twinkle, twinkle, little star, how I wonder what you are!" seems to have little relevance since Neil Armstrong walked on the moon. Yet, powerful as we are, we have not mastered death.

Death is still our greatest enemy, a mystery unresolved. It is what we fear the most. It is one of the most powerful realities that leads us into our journeys of powerlessness and sorrow.

Henry David Thoreau, famous American philosopher and poet, once said that every person really faces two deaths. There is the "biological death marked by mortuaries and monuments" and "spiritual death." Spiritual death, Thoreau concluded, often goes unnoticed but it is the "greater crisis" because it is avoidable —it requires a decision on our part.

Those who choose to worship Pumpkins, Drugs and other false gods choose to die spiritually. People who are addicted to drugs for example, alienate themselves from a personal, loving God. Their impersonal god—chemicals— becomes a substitute. It becomes their "best friend" to the degree they are willing to sacrifice their more intimate friends, family, freedom —everything they once valued that brought meaning and fulfillment. The result: spiritual death—separation from all that once filled their lives with spirit, meaning and joy.

Spiritual rebirth, life filled with meaning and growth, begins when we admit our powerlessness over our false gods and our sorrow. At that point we open our lives to a greater "spiritual reality": God. Letting go of the emotional and intellectual garbage our false gods give us, frees us to discover and experience a God of Greater Meaning.

Spiritual growth is essential to all human growth, according to Dr. Howard Clinebell, professor of counseling at the School of Theology at Claremont, California. He writes: "There is no way to 'fulfill' oneself except in relationship to the larger spiritual reality. By experiencing an intimate growing relationship with this reality, we connect with the Source of all growth and creativity."[2] This "Source of all growth and creativity," is what I choose to call the God of Greater Meaning.

Dr. Clinebell lists seven interrelated spiritual needs that are essential to our spiritual growth. They are:

  a. A viable (or enlivening) philosophy of life.
  b. A relationship with a loving God.
  c. Renewing moments of transcendence (moments with a God beyond us).
  d. A need for creative values.
  e. A need for developing our higher selves.
  f. A need for a trustful belonging in the universe.
  g. A need for a caring community that nurtures spiritual growth.[3]

All of the above spiritual needs are basic to and present in every person including those who are most alienated from institutional religions, Dr. Clinebell reports. And he concludes: "The satisfaction of those spiritual needs is essential for robust mental, physical and spiritual health. The goal of spiritual growth-work is learning how to satisfy the basic spiritual needs in growthful ways."[4]

Many people seek "growthful satisfaction" of the above spiritual needs in organized religions. However, Clinebell reports that in our growing secular culture where more and more people are feeling alienated from the organized church, many persons are seeking fulfilment of their spiritual needs outside religious institutions.

A vital, growing organization that is fulfilling the spiritual needs of persons more "secular" in thought is Alcoholic's Anonymous. The philosophy and Twelve Suggested Steps of A.A. are deeply spiritual and have helped thousands of recovering alcoholics and other persons addicted to drugs recover from their spiritual bankruptcy. According to the last unofficial report, there are now about 60 organizations using the Twelve Suggested Steps as a guide to spiritual recovery from other addictions like smoking, over-eating, gambling, work and emotions.

When we examine the Twelve Steps closely, we discover that they are related to God (steps 2, 3, 5, 6, 7 and 11), others (steps 5, 8, 9 and 12) and self (steps 1, 4, 5, and 10). The Twelve Suggested Steps help us live in harmony with God, self and others. (See Diagram #1 and Twelve Suggested Steps, Appendix.)

Living the philosophy of A.A. and the Twelve Suggested Steps not only helps the recovering alcoholic live in harmony with God, others and self, but also satisfies the seven spiritual needs essential to both his or her spiritual and human growth. The two work together.

If we live and practice the A.A. philosophy—"One day at a time.", "Easy does it.", "Let go and let God.", "Turn it over.", the Serenity Prayer and others—it fulfills the basic and essential spiritual need for a *viable (or enlivening) philosophy of life.*

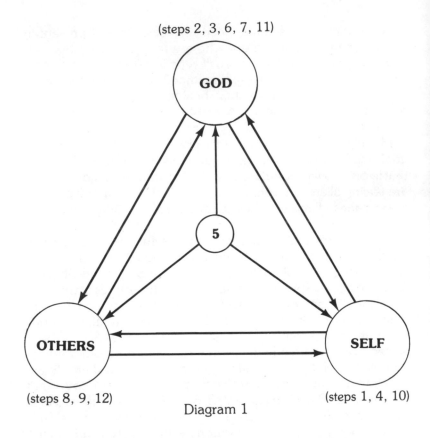

(steps 2, 3, 6, 7, 11)

GOD

5

OTHERS

SELF

(steps 8, 9, 12)

(steps 1, 4, 10)

Diagram 1

Steps 2, 3, 5, 6 and 7 fulfill our spiritual need to *live in harmony with a loving God*. If we admit that we are powerless over King Baby, drugs and other false gods we open ourselves to believe in a greater power who can restore us to sanity or wholeness (steps 1 & 2). Once we recognize the need for a greater power to help us out of our powerlessness, we can surrender our will and our lives to the care of that power (step 3). The Fifth Step helps us let go of character defects that block God's loving care. Steps 6 and 7 help us become entirely ready to have God remove all our defects of character and then humbly to ask God to do such.

Our spiritual need to have *renewed moments with a loving God* are fulfilled by working Step 11: "Sought through prayer and meditation to improve our conscious contact with God as we understood Him, praying only for knowledge of His will for us and the power to carry that out."

Two of our basic spiritual needs are fulfilled by working Steps 4, 5 and 10. If we take a searching and fearless, moral inventory of our lives (step 4) and admit to God, others and ourselves the exact nature of our wrongs (step 5) we will get in touch with our *creative values* and *develop our higher selves.* Steps 4 and 5 help us realize our real and greater values. Step 10, "Continued to take personal inventory and when we were wrong promptly admitted it.", helps us to stay in touch with our values and our higher selves. Working the above three steps helps build self-confidence and self-esteem.

Working four of the Twelve Suggested Steps fulfills our basic spiritual need for a *trustful.belonging in the universe.* Admitting to God, ourselves and another human being the "exact nature of our wrongs" (step 5), opens us to honest, trusting relationships with God, others and ourselves. By making a list of all persons we have harmed, becoming willing to make amends to them all (step 8) and then making direct amends to those people whenever possible (step 9), we will free ourselves from guilt and shame that blocks meaningful relationships with others. Step 12 helps us develop further trustful belonging in the universe by sharing our "spiritual awakening" with others and practicing all twelve step principles in "all our affairs."

Growth groups, A.A. meetings, aftercare, half-way homes, church support groups and worship experiences can provide us with *caring communities that nurture our spiritual growth,* our seventh and final spiritual need. (See Diagram 2 and Twelve Suggested Steps, Appendix.)

The A.A. philosophy and Twelve Suggested Steps are a universal guide for spiritual recovery from powerlessness and spiritual death. These steps, if worked faithfully, along with the A.A. philosophy, will help us let go of King Baby, drugs and other false gods which destroy our spiritual and human growth.

Furthermore, the Twelve Suggested Steps and A.A. philosophy help us overcome our greatest fear—powerlessness over dying and physical death. By living and practicing these "principles in all our affairs" we can honestly encounter the reality of physical death and dying because we will experience a God of Greater Meaning who can fulfill the sorrow in our lives and bring us joy.

In his masterful treatise on "The Meaning of Joy", Paul Tillich speaks of the fulfillment and joy we can achieve when we follow a spiritual guide like the one above. He writes:

> But only the fulfillment of what we really are can give us joy. Joy is nothing else than the awareness of our being fulfilled in our true being, in our personal center. And this fulfillment is possible only if we unite ourselves with what others really are. It is reality that gives joy, and reality alone. The Bible speaks so often of joy because it is the most realistic of all books. "Rejoice!" That means: "Penetrate from what *seems* to be real to that which is *really* real." Mere pleasure, in yourselves and in all other beings, remains in the realm of illusion about reality. Joy is born out of union with reality itself.[5]

A God of Greater Meaning can help us penetrate the illusion of our pleasure-giving, false gods and help us discover that which is *really* real—powerlessness, sorrow and joy!

STEPS:	SPIRITUAL NEEDS:
	a. Viable philosophy of life ("One day at a time." etc.).
(2, 3, 5, 6 & 7)	b. Relationship with a loving God.
(11)	c. Renewing moments with God.

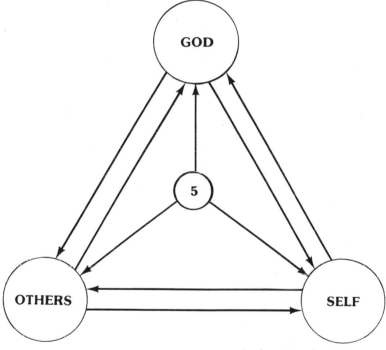

(5, 8, 9 & 12)

(1, 4, 5, & 10)

d. Creative values.
e. Develop our higher selves.
f. Trustful belonging in the universe.
g. Caring community that nurtures spiritual growth. (A.A. meetings, support groups, etc.).

Diagram 2

Notes

Chapter 1. King Baby Plays God
   1. Robert L. Short, *The Parable of Peanuts* (New York: Fawcett Crest, 1968) p. 49.
   2. Paul Tillich, *The New Being* (New York: Charles Scribner's Sons, 1955) p. 146.

Chapter 2. Pumpkins, Drugs and Other False Gods
   1. Tillich, p. 146.
   2. Ibid., p. 145.

Chapter 3. On Letting Go of King Baby
   1. John Powell, S.J., *A Reason To Live! A Reason to Die!* (Illinois: Argus Communications, 1972) p. 114.
   2. Eugene Kennedy, *The Joy of Being Human* (New York: Doubleday and Company, 1974), p. 322.

Chapter 4. On Letting Go of Pumpkins, Drugs and Other False Gods
   1. Powell, p. 53.

Chapter 5. Journey Into Powerlessness and Sorrow
   1. Powell, p. 112.
   2. Chicago Medicine, Vol. 76, No. 17, August 25, 1973, p. 661

Chapter 6. Journey Out: A Guide to Spiritual Recovery and a God of Greater Meaning
   1. Howard Clinebell, Growth Counseling, (Tennessee: Abingdon, 1979) p. 101.
   2. Ibid., p. 101.
   3. Ibid., p. 106.
   4. Ibid., p. 106.
   5. Tillich, p. 146.

Appendixes

The Twelve Steps of Alcoholics Anonymous

Step One: "We admitted we were powerless over alcohol —that our lives had become unmanageable."

Step Two: "Came to believe that a Power greater than ourselves could restore us to sanity."

Step Three: "Made a decision to turn our will and our lives over to the care of God as we understood Him."

Step Four: "Made a searching and fearless moral inventory of ourselves."

Step Five: "Admitted to God, to ourselves and to another human being, the exact nature of our wrongs."

Step Six: "Were entirely ready to have God remove all these defects of character."

Step Seven: "Humbly asked Him to remove our shortcomings."

Step Eight: "Made a list of all persons we had harmed, and became willing to make amends to them all."

Step Nine: "Made direct amends to such people whenever possible, except when to do so would injure them or others."

Step Ten: "Continued to take personal inventory and when we were wrong promptly admitted it."

Step Eleven: "Sought through prayer and meditation to improve our conscious contact with God as we understood Him, praying only for knowledge of His will for us and the power to carry that out."

Step Twelve: "Having had a spiritual awakening as the result of these steps, we tried to carry this message to alcoholics and to practice these principles in all our affairs."

For "Letting Go"

For a dear one about whom I have been concerned:

I behold the Christ in you.

I place you lovingly in the care of the
Father.

I release you from my anxiety and concern.

I let go of my possessive hold on you.

I am willing to free you to follow the
dictates of your own indwelling Lord.

I am willing to free you to live your
life according to your best light and
understanding.

Husband, wife, child, friend; I no longer
try to force my ideas on you, my ways
on you.

I lift my thoughts above you, above the
personal level.

I see you as God sees you, a spiritual
being, created in his image, and en-
dowed with qualities and abilities
that make you needed, and important . . .
not only to me, and my world, but to
God, and his larger plan.

I do not bind you. I no longer believe
that you do not have the understanding
you need in order to meet life.

I bless you; I have faith in you, I behold
the Christ in you.

—Anonymous

"I'd Pick More Daisies"

If I had my life to live over, I'd try to make more mistakes next time. I would be sillier than I have been this trip. I would relax. I would limber up. I know very few things I would take seriously. I would be crazier. I would be less hygienic. I would take more chances. I would take more trips. I would climb more mountains, swim more rivers, and watch more sunsets. I would burn more gasoline. I would eat more ice cream and less beans. I would have more actual troubles and fewer imaginary ones. You see I am one of the people who live prophylactically and sensibly and sanely, hour after hour, day after day.

Oh, I have my mad moments and if I had to do it over again, I'd have more of them; in fact, I'd try to have nothing else. Just moments, one after another, instead of living so many years ahead. I have been one of those people who never go anywhere without a thermometer, a hot water bottle, a gargle, a raincoat and a parachute. If I had to do it over again I would go places and travel lighter than I have.

If I had my life to live over again, I would start barefooted earlier in the Spring and stay that way later in the Fall. I would play hockey more. I would ride on more merry-go-rounds. I'D PICK MORE DAISIES.

— Anonymous

Reading Suggestions

William Glasser, *Positive Addiction.* New York: Harper and Row, 1976. Hardback. $7.95.

Eugene Kennedy, *If You Really Knew Me Would You Still Like Me?* Illinois: Argus Communications, 1975. Paperback. $2.25.

Eugene Kennedy, *The Joy of Being Human.* New York: Doubleday and Company, 1974. Paperback. $1.95.

George Mann, *Recovery of Reality.* New York: Harper and Row, 1979, Hardback, $8.95.

Clyde Reid, *Celebrate the Temporary.* New York: Harper and Row, 1972. Paperback. $1.95.

John Powell, S.J., *A Reason to Live! A Reason to Die!* Illinois: Argus Communications, 1972. Paperback. $2.95.

Robert Short, *Something to Believe In.* New York: Harper and Row, 1978. Paperback. $5.95.

William Miller, *You Count, You Really Do!* Minneapolis: Augsburg, 1976. Paperback. $3.50.